# PUNCHBOWL
## THE NATIONAL MEMORIAL CEMETERY OF THE PACIFIC

by Doug Carlson

An Island Heritage Book

*The beginning of the end*
*of War lies in Remembrance*
*Herman Wouk* *

PUNCHBOWL
The National Memorial Cemetery of the Pacific

Produced by
Island Heritage Publishing

Seventh Printing - 1989
Copyright © Island Heritage Publishing
Library of Congress Number 81-83482
ISBN 0-89610-085-5

Please address orders and editorial
correspondence to:
ISLAND HERITAGE PUBLISHING
*A Division of The Madden Corporation*
99-880 Iwaena Street
Aiea, Hawaii 96701
Phone: (808) 487-729

Printed in Hong Kong

First there is an enormous sense of quietude and peace, then a silence that thunders in the ears. The visitor is conscious of wind noises and the calling of birds. A great yellow Hawaiian sun lays a soft patina over the grave markers and the Garden of the Missing. There are flowers and shrubs, trees and grass — a feeling of deep reverence bound up in an enduring calmness.

And there is an awareness of time...

Ten million years ago the erupting top of a volcano broke the surface of the North Pacific Ocean. Wind-whipped, battered by waves and rain, the land persisted and remained, a bleak spot in a vast sea. More than a million years later another volcano appeared to the east, bursting out of the ocean in fiery creation to go through the same cycles of erosion, flowing lava and deep cracking of the land. In time, witnessed by no human eyes, the lava from the two volcanoes joined to form a larger island.

Along cracks in the land, new eruptions took place and the island grew and changed.

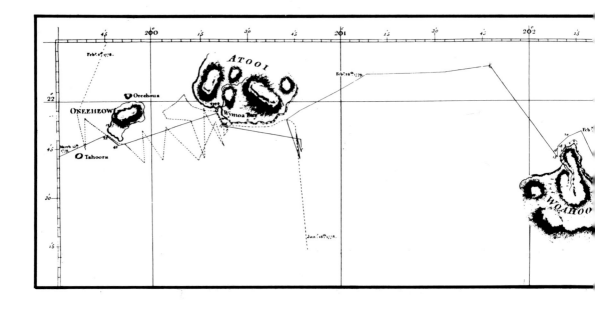

The sea around it rose and fell as great glaciers, thousands of miles away, formed and melted. The rising sea inundated much of the island, climbed at least 250 feet higher than now, then receded another 300 feet lower than the present shoreline. Some three million years ago the activity appeared to cease.

But a quarter of a million years ago the land cracked again in a north-south direction across a mountain chain. At the south end of the island, magma—underground molten lava—collided with rocks saturated with sea water and explosions broke out along the coral reef. The eruptions flattened the valley floor and built a series of tuff cones around the end of the island, cones of cinder and brown ash, characterized by their wide, saucer-shaped craters.

One of the tuff cones changed the topography of a valley and altered the course of streams. It was not as massive as its neighboring mountains but it was strategic, facing the deepwater harbor and looking down on plains to the east and west and the valley to the north.

Like the rest of the land, the cone waited for habitation. Birds came with seeds in their bellies; insects were blown thousands of miles, or washed in aboard living plants which rooted on hospitable shores. The island began to come alive and spawned an astonishing variety of species, as life forms adapted to either the low-lying areas or the heights that were often shrouded in rain or mist.

And still the island waited . . . .

Centuries passed. Then one day, on an island to the south, human feet stepped from canoes after an epic voyage, and human voices were added to the sound of the breaking surf and tradewinds. Human eyes

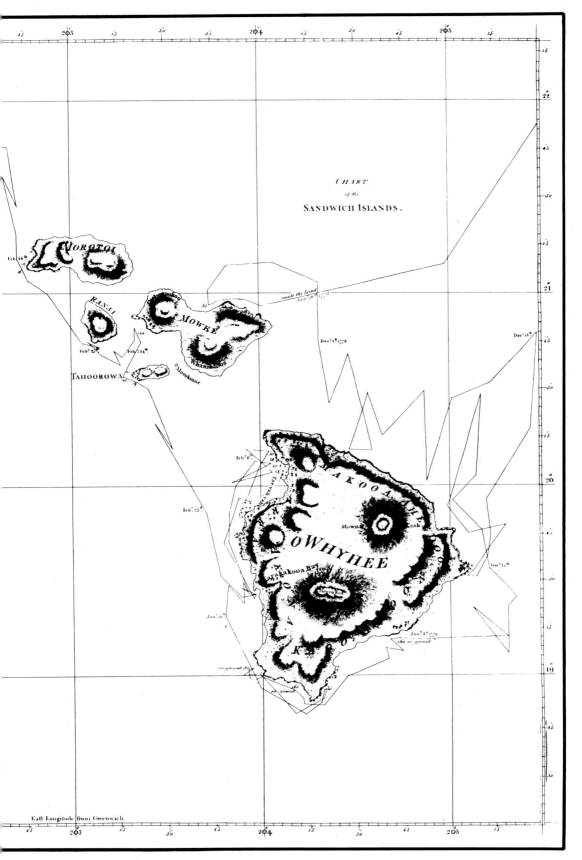

CHART
of the
SANDWICH ISLANDS.

MOROTOI

RANAI

MOWEE

TAHOOROWA

O Morokinne

made the land
Nov 26 1778

Dec 1st 1778

Dec 16th

Dec 20th

AKOOA HILL

Mowna Kaah

OWHYHEE

Kakooa Bay

Aina Roa

Jan 3d 1779
tho no ground

no ground tho

no ground

KA

East Longitude from Greenwich

5

Left: Fiery volcanic activity is still at work creating new land on the Big Island of Hawaii. Below: Early settlers made epic voyages in double-hull canoes to Hawaii. They are thought to have sailed from the Marquesas Islands.

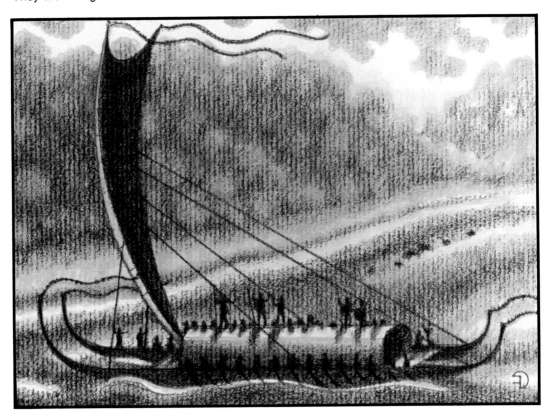

*looked for the first time on the beauty of the islands that lay at the apex of the Polynesian triangle, far north of other islands.*

*The colonizers moved through the island chain, bringing their gods and their glories, their splendors and their murders. They harvested the land as they had learned to harvest the sea and became highly specialized in their approach to the environment.*

*For one of the tuff cones, the one that sat in such a strategic place, they had a special use and a special name. They called it Puu O Waiho Ana, from which was derived Puowaina . . . the hill of placing, or laying up. The hill of sacrifice.*

The old generations called it Puowaina, and a street leading to the National Memorial Cemetery of the Pacific still bears that name. But today the Hill of Sacrifice is more commonly known as Punchbowl, and no one who has visited this round, gently sloping hill of volcanic origin need ask why.

In a world where the passing of time too often spells the obliteration of cultures and values, Punchbowl's significance has endured for countless generations. Puowaina is a bridge to the past, for it remains a hill of sacrifice in the 20th century just as it was a millennium ago.

For hundreds of years before Christian missionaries arrived in the Hawaiian Islands in 1820, Puowaina was the setting for human sacrifice, where fire consumed the bodies of men and women who had violated the "kapus" (tabus) of old Hawaii. From that fearsome past, Punchbowl crater has evolved to one of the world's greatest tributes to selfless sacrifice for one's country. More than two million people from North America, Japan and all over the world annually visit the National Cemetery here which has become an international symbol of honor, sacrifice and devotion to an ideal.

Where sacrificial fires once burned, visitors now overlook the cemetery and the city of Honolulu and its other world-famous landmark—Diamond Head crater, just beyond Waikiki.

Geologists tell us that Punchbowl was

created in a single day—perhaps in just a few hours—as superheated volcanic gas and steam tore through the earth, blasting mud, ash and rock into the air to form a nearly circular tuff cone. They even tell us with certainty which way the wind was blowing that day so many thousands of years ago. Punchbowl's highest elevation is on its southwest rim, which means the northeast tradewinds were blowing at the time of the eruption, just as they were when Diamond Head was created thousands of years later. Punchbowl's profile provides today's visitor with an ancient weather report contoured in earth and stone.

Just as Punchbowl was born of a cataclysmic event, the National Memorial Cemetery of the Pacific was born of another eruption on the earth's surface. This eruption lasted not one day, but well beyond a thousand. It, too, left its physical imprint on the landscape, but the deepest scars were left in the hearts of millions of people throughout the world.

The eruption that created the national cemetery was the Second World War.

For America that war began just 11 miles from Punchbowl—out beyond the airport toward Ewa town—at Pearl Harbor. Many of the 2,403 Americans who died on December 7, 1941, at Pearl, at Wheeler Air Field on Oahu's central plain and at the Kaneohe Marine Base on the windward side, now rest in Punchbowl. Among them is an unknown soldier whose remains were the first to be buried in the cemetery. Another is Lt. Hans C. Christiansen, a young Army flier killed early in the air attack and who is believed to be America's first combat victim of World War II in the Pacific.

Top: More than 2 million people visit
Punchbowl each year. Steps leading to
the War Memorial are flanked by the
Courts of the Missing, where marble
tablets record the names of 28,745 men
whose bodies were never recovered in
World War II, Korea and Vietnam. Left:
Sharp ridges of the Koolau Mountains
form a majestic backdrop to Punchbowl
crater. Above: Punchbowl's overlook
provides a sweeping view of Honolulu,
including Waikiki and world-famous
Diamond Head.

Punchbowl did not receive any of the dead from the war until nearly three and one-half years after the last shots were fired and the last bombs were dropped. Congress appropriated funds for the construction of the national cemetery in 1948, and the first interments were made on January 4, 1949.

Nearly 13,000 sons of Hawaii (then a Territory) and the nation were buried in private mass ceremonies during the next six months—hundreds in a single day. They were transferred here from temporary graves on Pacific islands and from mortuaries and cemeteries in Hawaii and on the Mainland. Public burials began on July 19, 1949—war correspondent Ernie Pyle was the first—and

Above: Despite the flow of visitors, Punchbowl can still be a place of solitude and serenity. Above right: Marble tablets in the Courts of the Missing. Right: Military units provide honor guards for interment ceremonies.

dedication ceremonies were held on the fourth anniversary of V-J day, September 2, 1949.

All together some 31,000 of America's dead from World War II are honored at Punchbowl, including 18,093 whose bodies were never recovered and whose names are inscribed on marble tablets in the Courts of the

ILLINOIS · LIEUTENANT(JG) · USNR · TEXAS
CLEVELAND JOHN RUFUS
VANIA · BOATSWAINS MATE 2C · USN · TEXAS

CLOUD GEORGE GRADY
VANIA · ENGINEMAN 1C · USN · CALIFORNIA
COALSON EDWARD J
EXICO · HOSPITAL CORPSMAN 1C · USN · NEW YORK
COBB HARLAN PAIGE
ERSEY · AIRMAN · USN · ALABAMA
COCHRAN BILLY EDWARD
ORNIA · LIEUTENANT(JG) · USN · PENNSYLVANIA
COFFMAN EMORY RONALD
SOURI · LT COMMANDER · USN · ALABAMA
COLEMAN ALFRED LEWIS
NSAS · FIREMAN · USN · MISSISSIPPI
COLEMAN RICHARD A
ORNIA · YEOMAN 3C · USN · MONTANA
COOK BAXTER HUGHES
YORK · LIEUTENANT(JG) · USN · TENNESSEE
COOK ORVILLE MELVIN
ONSIN · LIEUTENANT · USNR · ILLINOIS
COOK THEODORE AMOS
ORNIA · SEAMAN · USN · CALIFORNIA
CROSS RALPH
BAMA · LIEUTENANT(JG) · USN · IDAHO
CUMMINGS EDWARD P
STON · LIEUTENANT · USNR · NEW JERSEY
DACASTO LAURENCE J
UTAH · LIEUTENANT(JG) · USNR · CALIFORNIA
DAVENPORT HOWARD M JR
RNIA · LIEUTENANT(JG) · USN · NEW JERSEY

DAVIS ELTON RAYMOND
RSEY · AIRMAN · USN · CALIFORNIA
DAVIS ROY ANDERSON
OHIO · HOSPITAL CORPSMAN 1C · USN · KENTUCKY
DAVISWORTH JIMMY LEE
LINA · SEAMAN · USN · WEST VIRGINIA

Missing. All 1,102 who are entombed in the *U.S.S. Arizona* are listed here. The dead from World War II have been joined by 8,163 missing and 1,242 interred who died in Korea and another 2,489 missing and 213 buried whose lives ended in Vietnam.

From that first casualty of World War II to the last of the Vietnam conflict, surely none willingly sought or welcomed death. They cherished life every bit as much as the veterans of those wars who now make their solemn visits to Punchbowl to pause, to remember and to pray.

It has been said that "The beginning of the end of War lies in Remembrance."[1]

Punchbowl's simple beauty seems to make that remembrance all the more meaningful.

------

*It was a solemn moment. The kahunas (the priests) had left their home in Kewalo (now the site of McKinley High School in Honolulu) and had taken their victim down to the nearby pool, where they meant to kill him.*

*They expected his cooperation.*

*They reached the edge of the water and a priest stepped forward to urge the victim into the pool. The priest used a ritual chant—*

*"E moe malie i ka wai ko alii"*

*(Lie quietly in the waters of your chief).*

*The priests wanted an unblemished sacrifice, a victim unhurt and unmarked by struggling against his fate. Because he feared that if he resisted some other member of his family might be killed in his place, the victim stepped into the water without protest.*

*A priest leaned forward. In a few minutes it was over; a life had been taken.*

*The body of the drowned man was carried to a heiau (temple) near what is today the area of Lunalilo and Kinau streets. There, after a ceremony in the heiau, the priests assembled to bear the body up the Hill of Sacrifice.*

*They were a striking group. They wore white kepas, the garment that exposed one arm and shoulder, and white malos around their loins. Around their heads were bands of white tapa. They walked in silence, approached by no one.*

*At the top of the hill they placed the body on a great altar stone on which were smaller stones forming an "imu ahi," a fire oven. They kindled a fire and the natural draft of the wind among the stones quickly fed the blaze.*

*It was early morning. At dawn the smoke could be seen over Puowaina, but the priests had gone, and there was only the smoke, the breeze and the sudden sunrise.*

*That night the family of the victim went up to the altar stone and claimed the remains of the sacrifice.*

*Not all of the bodies were burned. Some were left for the families to claim, intact and unmarked. Some were left to decompose.*

*The victims had broken a kapu, one of the rigid rules of conduct for which the penalty was death. There was no appeal because there was no misunderstanding of the law. The kapu system, with its sacrifices, reached back into antiquity, and it would reach forward*

[1] *War and Remembrance*, © 1978 by Herman Wouk.

*some years after the coming of the haoles—*
*the foreigners in the tall, white ships.*

---

The history of ancient Hawaii has been transmitted through the generations by chants and legends. The Hawaiians had no written language before the 19th century, when Christian missionaries brought their God to these islands.

Western cultures place great emphasis on the written word and tend to denigrate oral histories, as if the written word were more valid than the spoken. But the Hawaiians had no other way to keep their culture alive over

In the religion of ancient Hawaii, those who violated the strict kapus governing daily life could be sentenced to death. Their bodies would be carried to the sacrificial rock on the rim of Puowaina—the Hill of Sacrifice.

the centuries. A chant to the Hawaiians contained as much truth as a parchment, scroll or book to other cultures.

Children were selected at an early age for their destiny as a chanter, to sit at the feet of the old ones, memorizing legends that could last for hours or even days. And so the legends of Hawaii are more than amusements, and the stories told by the old Hawiians in the 19th century were recorded, studied and compared for similarities and verification.

Such was the case with the legends of Puowaina and its history as a place for human sacrifice. The stories have survived:

*"Kewalo (was) a fishpond and surrounding land on the plains below King Street, and beyond Koula. It contains a spring rather famous in the times previous to the conversion to Christianity, as the place where victims designed for the heiau of Kanelaau on Punchbowl slopes were first drowned..."* [2]

*"The bodies of those slain for breaking the tabu were laid on the altar-like ledge at the top and burned, the crack below giving a good draught of air."* [2]

*"The great stone on the top of Punchbowl Hill was the place for the burning (of) men."* [2]

That "great stone" of sacrifice survived into the 20th century and became a popular lookout for hikers and motorists who ventured up the rutted dirt road to the rim of Punchbowl. Eventually the stone was excavated to make way for the concrete overlook on the crater's rim above Honolulu.

Visitors today pause for a magnificent view of the city and the cemetery below, standing on a once-sacred spot where only priests and their retinue once trod bearing their sacrifices.

---

*Flushed with victory and bent on destroying his remaining enemies, the young king from the island of Hawaii swept through the chain of islands and stood, at last, against the only significant opposition left to him, the army of Oahu.*

*That army was ably commanded by Kaiana and under the overall supervision of the king of Oahu, Kalanikupule. But in facing the vehement force from Hawaii Island, the Oahu legions were facing a meteoric commander-*

Left: The "great stone" of sacrifice provided a popular lookout for hikers and motorists before it was excavated to make room for today's overlook. Above: Historical accounts say some of Punchbowl's sacrificial victims were drowned in a fishpond at Kewalo. This fishpond, photographed around 1912, was not far from Punchbowl (background) or present-day Kewalo Street.

[2]Sterling, Elspeth P., *Sites of Oahu* rev. ed., Honolulu, Dept. of Anthropology, Dept. of Education, Bernice P. Bishop Museum. 1978.

in-chief, a king who would not be turned aside. History would call him "The Napoleon of the Pacific"—Kamehameha.

And there was more. Kamehameha's forces were loyal and fired with a sense of destiny. They also had foreign mercenaries in the form of John Young and his companions. Young, a British seaman, had joined forces with Kamehameha and taught his followers the rudiments of European military drill and tactics, and had supplied some firearms to augment the Hawaiian spears and warclubs.

The two armies clashed in the area below Puowaina, near the heiau at Kanelaau, in the vicinity of the present Kinau, Alapai and Lunalilo streets. The battle was fought along a line of heiau outposts which guarded the heiau of Puowaina.

The Oahu forces began to fall back, only to collide with a segment of Kamehameha's army which had poured through the pass at Papakolea, near Puowaina. A battle raged through Pauoa Valley, and a retreat by the Oahu forces continued through nearby Nuuanu Valley and, inexorably, toward the Pali, the high cliff of the Koolau mountain range which separates windward and leeward Oahu.

The retreating army paused at Elekoki, a pool on Nuuanu Stream. But the end was near. Kaiana, the Oahu army commander, fell in combat. The Oahu king, Kalanikupule, dropped from a gunshot wound and was carried to a heiau where he died. The retreat went farther up the valley.

Under the command of Nahili a portion of the Hawaii Island army forced the last of Kalanikupule's followers as far as they could go, where they leaped to their deaths to avoid capture. Kamehameha's hold on Oahu was secured, as was his place in history. The last remaining island, Kauai, pledged its loyalty and Kamehameha ruled in name and in fact. In the decisive battle that began near Puowaina, the course of Hawaiian history was changed forever.

---

Kamehameha's bloody victory gained on the slopes of Punchbowl and in the far reaches of Nuuanu Valley brought to an end the generations-old warfare in Hawaii. Honolulu's small merchant community prospered in the peace of Kamehameha's rule, and tall-masted sailing ships competed for space in the

Left: View of Honolulu Harbor from Punchbowl in 1900.
Top: Hawaiians entertain a visitor at their home in Punchbowl
crater, about 1908. Above: Kamehameha the Great, who conquered
and united the Hawaiian Islands.

Below: Undated photograph shows Punchbowl's sacrificial rock and the neglected cannons that once guarded Honolulu Harbor from the crater's rim. Right: Gentle rains blow often over the cemetery from the Koolau Mountains. Even in the 19th century, Punchbowl was a popular picnic spot.

natural harbor. Lookouts positioned on Punchbowl's rim signaled the approach of vessels to the busy port below.

The arrival of those ships and all that came with them changed Hawaii forever. The Hill of Sacrifice was used less for that purpose than for its military strategic overlook of the harbor, although accounts survive of a sacrifice that occurred as late as 1809.

But for the people of 19th century Honolulu, Punchbowl became a destination for pleasant daytrips to picnic and view the changing scene below. As the small town of Honolulu pushed back its outskirts and homes with fine views were built on the gentle lower slopes of the extinct volcano, a canopy of trees gradually spread throughout the town on what had once been a barren plain.

The proliferation of all this foliage was not by accident, as the civic-minded among the populace were encouraged to help with the "greening" of Honolulu. Tree planting even extended to the interior of Punchbowl itself, as described in an 1875 newspaper account of King Kalakaua's efforts:

"During the past fortnight His Majesty the King set his subjects a good example which we could hope to see extensively followed throughout the islands; we refer to tree-planting. Daily the King, accompanied often by the Queen and other members of the Royal Family, and surrounded by scores of men, women and children may have been seen heavily engaged in the work of laying out and planting a park of trees on the top of Punchbowl hill."

According to the account, the king and his court planted ingas, acasias, algerobas, eucalypti and other varieties in circular rows, with space enough between for carriage paths.

The people did come by carriage, by horse and by foot, including Honolulu's early tourists—those who traveled to the Islands only for the experience, and not for financial gain and what could be taken from the land and waters of Hawaii. Once at Punchbowl's summit, 578 feet above the sea, the 19th century visitor saw open fields, fishponds and large stands of coconut trees, as described in the magazine *Paradise of the Pacific* in 1892:

"Off to the left a long ridge of land terminating in picturesque Diamond Head, 762 feet high, bounds the view. The sweep of the beach at Waikiki is marked by the long lines of coconut trees growing there. Then comes on the shore and beyond the squares of "Salt Pans" dug in the marsh. Further along is the saluting battery, and then the cluster of buildings which form the Immigration Depot. A little way from this we will probably see a vessel drawn up on the Marine Railway, and a short distance seaward the entrance to the harbor, with the sun breaking on the coral reef on each side of the channel. Across the channel is a low sand spit on which is the Quarantine Station, and inshore of this sandy flat is a shallow stretch of water which extends as far as Pearl River Harbor, the three lochs of which, eleven miles distant, glitter in the sun.

"Beyond Pearl River the beach trends away in the distance to Barber's Point, about fifty

**19**

miles away. The beautiful range of the Waianae mountains, 4,000 feet high, rises shrouded in a warm, soft purplish haze.

"In the middle distance, between the Waianae range and the mountains behind of us, of which Punchbowl is an out-lying crater, is a broad plain, over which we ride if we take a trip 'Around the Island.' We can trace the windings of the road leading from Pearl River, the little settlement at the head of which is called Ewa ("Ava"), and as the eye follows it into town we see that it passes close to Oahu Prison, the only one on the islands. Around the prison are some large fish-ponds, and near them the Kalihi, Nuuanu, and Pauoa Valley streams find their way into the harbor.

"As for the city itself it is so tree-embowered, that only the roofs of some of the loftiest buildings and the spires of the churches, and the numerous flagstaffs are to be seen. Behind and on either hand rise the high peaks of the range of mountains dividing this part of the island. The loftiest peak, on the south of the Pali road is 3100 feet high, Lanihuli peak on the north side, 2780. Tantalus, over Punahou, 2013. Olympus, over Manoa valley (and Oahu College of course), 2447.

"The visitor to the top of Punchbowl will probably notice that the interior of that crater is thickly covered with the Algeroba tree. These as well as the trees on the hill to the left have been set out to test the question as to whether many of the barren hills on the islands cannot be crowned with fruit trees and the experiments have succeeded well. To illustrate what can be done in this volcanic black sand, it may be mentioned that when in 1820, the first missionaries landed in Honolulu, there was hardly a tree or shrub to be seen on the plain, where the city now stands."

---

*Following the decisive battle that raged from Puowaina to the Pali, the military and strategic significance of Puowaina was well understood and appreciated.*

*The British mercenary, John Young, was intrigued with the hill's possiblities in terms of firepower. As Kamehameha's military advisor, Young had to be concerned about possible enemies, among whom he numbered the Russians.*

*The Russians had cast a covetous eye on the Hawaiian Islands, knowing their mid-Pacific location would be a strategic and economic asset to whoever controlled them. Young suspected the Russians of trying to establish a*

*colony on the northwesterly island of Kauai that would be a prelude to more encroachment. He felt the Russians' motives were more sinister than mere support of their sandalwood trade.*

*About 1816 Young ordered eight heavy guns placed on Puowaina, positioning them atop the hill facing the harbor. At the same time he built a fort near the harbor and armed it with cannons, all as a deterrent to what he considered a potential threat. Young had started a precedent that would outlast him.*

*Some thirty years after Young's precautions, the cannon battery atop the hill was called Fort Punchbowl, reportedly with eleven guns and 33 men assigned. In time the number would be reduced to two guns used for ceremonial purposes.*

*Once when they were not fired it caused a*

*controversy and aroused criticism of a king.*

*The king was Kalakaua, new to the throne as successor to Liholiho. Kalakaua defied tradition and refused to allow the guns on Punchbowl to be fired in Liholiho's memory. It was a blatant attempt to negate Liholiho's popularity and Kalakaua was roundly criticized by local newspapers.*

*In 1895 the guns were fired, this time in anger. It was in the last gasp that marked the end of the monarchy era and the beginning of a new and modern Hawaii. The conflict was between Royalist supporters of that magnificent lady, Queen Liliuokalani, and the supporters of a Hawaiian republic.*

*Captain Samuel Nowlein, who had commanded segments of the Queen's guards, took matters into his own hands and led a contingent against a small force of republi-*

Cemetery above a city, Punchbowl lies in the heart of Honolulu, itself the hub of the Pacific. Local government has enacted special zoning to prevent further high-rise development near the crater.

Below: A 1920s Easter sunrise service on Punchbowl's summit. Near right: Floodlights on Iolani Palace illuminated the cross from below. Far right: Punchbowl's Easter tradition continues, and high school students now have the honor of erecting the cross.

cans who were atop Puowaina. The republican forces responded with 15 shells from the Punchbowl cannons, the barrage trapping Nowlein's men in a volcanic pocket and threatening them with annihilation. Nowlein surrendered. The strategic importance of Punchbowl had been demonstrated once again. No one at the time could guess it was for the last time.

Queen Liliuokalani was destined to be the last reigning Hawaiian monarch. Hawaii was formally annexed to the United States in 1900 and became a state of the Union in 1959.

---

The idea of putting a cemetery in Punchbowl crater originated in the late 1890s during the years between the overthrow of the Hawaiian monarchy and annexation by the United States. A committee was formed to select a suitable site for a new cemetery to serve the fast-growing town of Honolulu. Inevitably, Puowaina—the Hill of Sacrifice—was proposed for its unique combination of accessibility and its sense of sublime isolation.

Opposition soon arose, however, based upon apparent real concern for public health and an ill-defined emotional objection. In April of 1899, William T. Bringham, director of the Bernice Pauahi Bishop Museum in Honolulu, predicted that burial and decomposition of human remains in Punchbowl would spoil the city's water supply by contamination through the rifts and cracks in the crater.

Noting his objection to the already established cemetery in the nearby Makiki district, Bringham cautioned, "... but while a few graves may not pollute the water supply

Above: The first light of an Easter sunrise. Above right: A child is remembered at Easter. Dependents also may be buried in national cemeteries.

to an intolerable extent, it is to be feared that a hundred acres packed with rotting corpses in the very funnel of this volcano will in time menace public health." Bringham concluded with the observation that the ancient Romans had allowed no burials within the city walls and that Honolulu would do well in her tropical climate to borrow that Roman wisdom.

The emotional objection to a Punchbowl cemetery was simply stated: "It is very undesirable to have a cemetery—a city of the dead, so to say—above a city of the living." Both this psychological aversion and the professed concern for the public health were to surface nearly 50 years later as objections to the creation of the National Memorial Cemetery of the Pacific.

But for most of those 50 years, Punchbowl continued to serve Honolulu's population principally as a park, a saucer of open space to the mountains, sea and sky. New uses intruded: the National Guard maintained a marksmanship range inside the crater, while on the outside slopes an ever-increasing number of homes were built to take advantage of one of the world's great views.

An annual function at Punchbowl that today attracts thousands of visitors and residents had its origins in a moment of teenage exuberance experienced by five boys around 1910. The boys lived not far from Punchbowl and used the volcano's summit as their own hideaway.

Shortly before Easter one year, they talked with their Sunday School teacher about the beauty of their hilltop retreat and suggested that they hold the next Easter sunrise service on the crater rim. The service conducted by a class and teacher from the first Portuguese Protestant Mission in Hawaii, later known as the Pilgrim Church, was not long—just two favorite hymns and the reading of the 121st Psalm. But it was the beginning of an annual celebration undertaken in the early years by enthusiastic volunteers and since 1918 by the Hawaii Council of Churches.

In 1926 students from McKinley High School on the flat plain below Punchbowl revived an ancient Hawaiian custom that had been used to build the old heiaus (temples). Their purpose just before Easter that year,

Below: The *Arizona* Memorial at Pearl Harbor spans the sunken battleship. Names of the 1,102 men entombed below are inscribed on marble tablets in Punchbowl's Courts of the Missing. Right: December 7, 1941. The *U.S.S. Shaw*, sitting in drydock, explodes from direct hits by Japanese bombs.

however, was to build a platform on Punchbowl's rim to support the Easter cross.

According to newspaper reports of the day, 2,000 students formed a human chain from their school on King Street to the top of Punchbowl. In just over an hour the students passed 100 large stones hand-to-hand up Puowaina's slopes to the rim overlooking their school and the city, where they were deposited with other rocks brought by truck to form the overlook platform.

In the years to come, Punchbowl's Easter cross would rest there, bathed in searchlights from below and illuminated brightly enough to be seen by approaching ships far beyond the calm waters of Honolulu Harbor.

Although the early proposal to construct a cemetery within Punchbowl was not adopted, the idea was never forgotten by Hawaii's war veterans. Throughout the years following the Great War, veterans campaigned for the establishment of a national cemetery in the Territory. Led principally by the American Legion, Hawaii's veterans repeatedly urged approval of the plan in their letters and resolutions to Washington.

That decades-long effort finally produced results—at least on paper—in November 1941 when Congress authorized the expenditure of $50,000 for the creation of a national cemetery in Hawaii, provided that the land be made available to the federal government at no cost.

That approval, coming when it did, was a chilling prophecy of what lay ahead for Hawaii, the nation and a generation of her young men.

---

*In December 1940 the tough little Japanese admiral revealed to his staff plans he had made for an attack on the U.S. Pacific Fleet, headquartered at Pearl Harbor, Oahu, in the Hawaiian Islands. "Operation Z" was Admiral Isoroku Yamamoto's deeply-held secret, but once made known it launched a series of events that culminated in the actual attack on December 7, 1941.*

*Only a month after Yamamoto's plans were outlined for the Japanese Navy, the U.S. Ambassador to Japan, Joseph Grew, reported a rumor that the Japanese were planning a surprise attack on Pearl Harbor. His report failed to cause any great stir, at least not enough to raise the state of readiness in Hawaii to a proper level.*

*Through the ensuing months of negotiations, diplomatic maneuvering and high-level talks, the defenders of Pearl Harbor remained*

Left: Early-morning visitors arrive for Veterans Day observance. Flags donated by relatives of deceased veterans form "Avenue of the Flags" on Presidents Day, Independence Day, Veterans Day and Thanksgiving. Below: Veteran of a war fought long ago honors the fallen.

*unconvinced that they would see a major attack, and they were equally unaware of the Japanese task force that had sailed in secret in late November from a base in Japan's remote northern islands.*

*At 7:55 a.m., Hawaii time, Japanese carrier-launched Aichi, Nokajima and Mitsubishi aircraft began an attack against the Pacific Fleet and military installations on Oahu. It had been a calm Sunday morning, but in the shattering surprise attack, America was hurled into World War II. The Day of Infamy was a prelude to an ultimate day of reckoning.*

*But not that Sunday morning. That terrible day saw the deaths of 2,335 U.S. military men and 68 civilians, the destruction of hundreds of U.S. aircraft and the sinking or damaging of 18 ships.*

*Considering the level of readiness, the response of the defenders was remarkable. But defense strategies—perhaps because of years of tradition—had assumed any attack*

Above: Construction of the National Cemetery began in 1948 after a decades-long effort to win approval in Congress. Right: Army, Navy, Air Force and Marine honor guards stand at ease prior to Veterans Day ceremony.

*against the Islands would be from the sea. Consequently, the guns of Punchbowl had been placed to defend against a coastal attack, and were ineffective against attacking aircraft. The nature of warfare had changed and, for the first time, Punchbowl's strategic position was of little value.*

*Punchbowl's gun batteries did not fire a shot during the Pearl Harbor attack, nor at any time thereafter in World War II.*

The war that erupted in sudden fury at Pearl Harbor eventually would send thousands of America's battle dead to their final resting place in Punchbowl, just 11 miles from where it began in a horror of billowing smoke, sinking ships and drowning men.

That final rest would not be secured at Punchbowl until more than seven years after that Day of Infamy, and the national cemetery would await dedication until the fourth anniversary of the victory over Japan.

It was military necessity—not a lack of

concern for the dead—that caused the repeated delays in creating a place for their final interment. This issue, like so many others, was set aside while attention and resources were focused on rebuilding the fleet, assembling the manpower and winning the war.

The early days of the war, however, did produce an effort to designate Punchbowl as the national cemetery site in Hawaii. The Army published a general order just three weeks after the December 7th attack to that effect, but it was rescinded less than a month later due to strong objections by the National Guard, which used the crater for its small arms marksmanship and other training.

Hawaii's veterans nevertheless continued their efforts on behalf of the Punchbowl cemetery and succeeded in having the Territorial Legislature pass a resolution in 1943 requesting the governor to make Punchbowl available to the federal government. No action was taken, however, and it became increasingly apparent that a cemetery would

not be built until after the war's end.

Meanwhile, the thousands of Americans who were dying in the Pacific war were interred near the spot where they fell, in ill-defined cemeteries where later recovery efforts became detective work. The temporary resting places for young soldiers, sailors and Marines had unfamiliar names to their countrymen—New Caledonia, Tutuila in the Samoan Islands, Wake, Christmas and Canton Islands and many others. Here they remained until a prodigious effort was begun by Congressional direction in 1946 to repatriate the World War II dead.

In Hawaii most of the Navy's dead—except those who were entombed within the *Arizona*—were buried at a newly established naval cemetery in Halawa, on a hill overlooking the harbor. The Army designated the Schofield Barracks Cemetery as the temporary interment site for the majority of deceased Army personnel.

Even after the end of hostilities on Septem-

Right: The dead of World War II who were to be interred in Punchbowl were brought to Hawaii from overseas cemeteries. Their caskets were prepared at Pearl Harbor's mausoleum for burial. Below: Hundreds of GIs, almost all of them from the Mainland, were interred daily from January to July 1949. The general public was not permitted into the cemetery during these early months. Below right: Construction work continued as this young Marine stood his post of honor just prior to interment rites.

ber 2, 1945, the proposal to create a national cemetery at Punchbowl did not receive urgent consideration until the body repatriation program had begun, with all its attendant problems caused by the magnitude of the operation.

Early in 1947 Army headquarters authorized the Western Division Engineer in Hawaii to begin the planning for a Punchbowl cemetery. Congressional efforts also intensified at that time to obtain an appropriation for the cemetery, and Hawaii delegate to Congress Joseph R. Farrington solicited unified support from local governmental officials.

Again, as in the late 1890s, objections to a Punchbowl cemetery arose that its presence would contaminate the city's water supply. No less an authority than the manager and chief engineer of the Board of Water Supply told the City Planning Commission a cemetery in the crater "could become a great mistake, insofar as its possible sanitary and psychological effect upon the future of Honolulu's water supply is concerned."

But unlike the decision of a half-century before, Punchbowl this time was considered not to be a health hazard in the final decision by local officials. They deferred to the opinion of the Territorial Board of Health that Punchbowl was "composed of material that would not be favorable for seepage of pollution into our water supply basin."

Strong pleas were made for the cemetery by representatives of veterans organizations and by the military itself, under the pressing necessity to provide permanent burial for the more than 9,000 bodies of servicemen stored above ground in mausoleum warehouses in Hawaii, as well as another 9,500 on Guam awaiting burial instructions.

The long-awaited major step for creation of the cemetery was achieved on February 24, 1948, when the House Appropriations Committee approved legislation that included funds for the cemetery. Final Congressional action was completed shortly thereafter.

Construction began in August 1948, and planning intensified to handle the burial of thousands of Americans in Punchbowl, a task that required the precision of a military operation as well as the sensivity and dignity

of a funeral service. One of the key decisions made at this time was to use flat grave markers in the cemetery rather than crosses or Stars of David as the permanent headstones, in order to reduce the appearance of crowding. That decision was consistent with Department of the Army policy regarding national cemeteries. A later decision to erect wooden crosses and Stars of David temporarily above the graves until the flat markers were on hand ultimately sparked a controversy that would lead all the way to the White House before it was put to rest.

In June 1948 the Office of the Quartermaster General in Washington directed that all interments in overseas cemeteries (which would include Hawaii) would be closed to the next of kin and the public. The decision was reached no doubt in part because of the sensitivity of conducting mass burials in the overseas cemeteries. Local military authorities objected to the directive, noting that Hawaii's next of kin had been told they could attend the interment rites of their dead. And, too, it was recognized that some next of kin could be expected to travel from the Mainland for the

rites and to deny their attendance at the ceremonies would be unreasonable. The directive finally was lifted and the opening of the cemetery for public burials was scheduled for July 19, 1949.

But even with the delay of interment for some of the deceased, the central fact faced by planners of the new cemetery was the vast number of war dead awaiting burial. Thousands of bodies already were in mausoleums on Oahu and others were arriving from Guam and other Pacific locations during the early phases of construction. Notwithstanding the number to be buried each day, the dignity of the ceremony had to be preserved. The planners ultimately established a three-day cycle for the interments that they believed met the requirements for speed and efficiency and for the respect due to America's war dead.

On the first day of the cycle the caskets scheduled for interment were set aside at the distribution center and were draped with flags tagged with name and rank. On that same day at the cemetery, engineers surveyed the burial site and put down lines for the next day's trenching operation.

On the second day the flags were removed from the caskets at the distribution center and were placed in cellophane envelopes. The caskets were loaded on trailer beds, 18 on each trailer, and stacked two high. Trenching machines were employed at the cemetery to prepare enough trench lines to accommodate the interments the following day. The location of each grave was pegged at the bottom of the five-foot trenches.

At 6:30 a.m. on the day of the burials, the trailers left the distribution center under military and police escort for the drive to the cemetery. Cranes were used to remove the caskets from the trailers and to place them next to the trenches by 9 a.m., by which time the location of each casket had been recorded on a master list. A ceremonial detachment had placed each tagged flag, still folded in the cellophane bag, on the appropriate casket.

All construction work in Punchbowl was stopped as one casket was chosen arbitrarily and its flag held taut above it by four military honor guard. A Protestant, a Jewish and a Catholic clergyman read their respective burial service, after which three rifle volleys were fired and a bugler sounded taps. The flag was refolded and presented to an officer, who accepted it on behalf of all next of kin. The ceremony was over.

Flags were gathered from the other caskets and returned to the distribution center for shipment to the next of kin. After the entire trench was filled with caskets, lowered one at a time, bulldozers filled in the trench with dirt, which was tamped by hand and machine.

The operation was complete. The dead of World War II had reached their resting place.

At 11 a.m. on January 4, 1949, the first burial service at the National Memorial Cemetery of the Pacific was read over the coffin of an unknown serviceman who had died on December 7, 1941. One-hundred and eight others were also buried that day, the same number buried on the second and third day of interments. The rate soon increased to 216 daily as called for by the contractor's specifications.

During the first phase of interments from January 4 to March 25, the remains of 9,940 Americans were buried at Punchbowl. They represented nearly all who were available for interment at the time. In the following months more dead became available for burial, and the second major phase of interments began on June 13. Another 1,778 were interred in that group by June 23, including many who had been brought to Hawaii from their temporary graves at Wake Island and Formosa.

No markers were placed at the graves immediately after the interments. Grave locations had been recorded, and since the public had not yet been admitted in any numbers to the cemetery, no pressing need was felt to erect the markers.

With the approach of the July 19 public opening, however, authorities ordered wooden crosses out of stockpiles; Stars of David were on requisition. The markers were in poor condition, and all required painting before they could be erected, but by July 18 markers were in place over all graves that had been filled before June 13.

On July 19, 1949, the cemetery's gates were opened to the general public. At 9:30 services were held for five war dead—an unknown serviceman, two young Marines, an Army lieutenant and a middle-aged veteran of World War I. He was a war correspondent who covered one battle too many: Ernie Pyle.

*John Donne wrote that "any man's death diminishes me, for I am involved in mankind." The death of Ernest Taylor Pyle, whose remains lie in the grandeur of Punchbowl today, diminished millions of his*

readers, for he gave the world a new way of looking at war and the men who fought it.

Ernie Pyle was a famous war correspondent and more—he was the chronicler of the doughboy, the dogface, the grunt, the average infantryman from smalltown America. He wrote more about privates than generals. He was more familiar with foxholes than headquarters. He never glamorized war for he saw it clearly, and he wrote about it in simple and forceful prose.

He was a favorite of the GIs everywhere and he went through some rough campaigns with them. He once wrote that "I don't want to come home until I can come home for good," and it was prophetic. Like thousands of other Americans, Ernie Pyle would die in combat.

It was April 18, 1945, on the island of Ie Shima, only ten miles square, in what was almost a denouement of the war. He had rolled out of a jeep to escape the gunfire from a Japanese Nambu machine gun. The gunner had let several vehicles pass, then opened up on the jeep carrying Ernie and four others. They went into a ditch alongside the road, but by then the gunner had time to adjust his sights and he fired a burst at the ditch. Ernie Pyle was struck in the left temple and died instantly.

He was buried on Ie Shima underneath a crude marker that read:

*At this spot*
*The 77th Infantry Division*
*Lost a Buddy*
*ERNIE PYLE*
*18 April 1945*

*After the war the remains were moved, first to an Army cemetery on Okinawa, then to Punchbowl. His grave marker is there, no different from the thousands of markers that note the final resting places for other Americans who died in battle. To be surrounded in*

Above left: Honolulu Cub Scouts honor Ernie Pyle each Memorial Day by decorating his grave with dozens of flower leis. Above: Wooden crosses and Stars of David were erected temporarily in the cemetery until flat, ground-level markers could be installed. Removal of the crosses in 1951 sparked a national furor.

*lasting peace by the men he immortalized, the extraordinary ordinary men—Ernie Pyle would have asked no more than that.*

---

"Anybody who has been in a war and wants to go back is a plain damn fool in my book. I'm going simply because I've got to . . . and I hate it."

Those words were written by Ernie Pyle after he had seen more than his share of European war and just before he shipped out to the Pacific. Those two sentences say it all; they explain his appeal to GIs and the folks back home. Ernie Pyle's stories for the Scripps-Howard newspaper chain were simple, blunt and honest.

His death was mourned across America, in foxholes, ships and tanks, among American fighting men the world over. President Truman's statement on Ernie's death said: "No man in this war has so well told the story of the American fighting man as American fighting men wanted it to be told. He deserved the gratitude of all his countrymen."

Ernie Pyle's interment on the first morning of public ceremonies at the National Memo-rial Cemetery of the Pacific was an expression of that gratitude for this 45-year-old Pulitzer Prize-winning correspondent and World War I veteran from Indiana.

On that bright, blue-sky morning of July 19, 1949, Ernie was eulogized before a crowd of 2,000 as the "GIs reporter," and then was laid to rest with four GIs representing all those he wrote about. An orchid and rose quill was placed near the grave by a newspaperman "as the press' salute to Ernie— and to every newsman killed while trying to tell the story of World War II."

Since that day millions have visited the simple grave of Ernie Pyle, who more than likely would be embarrassed by all the attention. But the "GI's reporter" would probably also smile to know that two Unknowns from World War II were right there beside him to share in all the fuss.

The pace of burials at Punchbowl was slower now, befitting the nature of the public ceremonies attended by families and friends of Hawaii's war dead. Almost all of the nearly 400 who were interred during the next five weeks were native sons of Hawaii, most of

them young Japanese-Americans who had proven their loyalty to the United States of America by their heroism in the European theater of war. The 442nd Regimental Combat Team and the 100th Battalion—the two Japanese-American, all-volunteer combat units—not only were among the most decorated fighting units in the entire United States Army but also sustained some of the heaviest casualties of the war with their "Go For Broke" determination to accomplish the mission, whatever the cost.

These young heroes of Hawaii finally had come home to lie in their native soil.

The Army, which was responsible for construction of the cemetery, had held out hope for dedication early in the summer, but sections of Punchbowl's floor remained too raw and unfinished. It was decided to open the cemetery to the public, undedicated, rather than delay the interment of Hawaii's dead any longer. The planners then settled upon the earliest date of historical importance for the dedication—September 2, 1949, the fourth anniversary of Victory over Japan Day. It also represented the first anniversary

Punchbowl has aged gradually since the time when crosses stood on the graves. The growth of Honolulu—and particularly Waikiki in the distance—has been much more dramatic.

of ceremonies honoring the initial large shipment of Hawaii's war dead to be returned home.

The several thousand guests who attended the dedication entered the cemetery by the same road as the modern visitor, but the sight that greeted them was much different than today. At the head of each grave was erected a white cross or Star of David in rows that created diagonal and parallel patterns in the dazzling sunlight. It was a stunning sight, one that many seemed to expect in a national cemetery.

**41**

Above: February 2, 1956—Nineteen "unknowns" from the Korean Conflict are interred. All American casualties from Korea who could not be identified are buried at Punchbowl. Above right: Each of the nearly 28,000 graves is decorated with flower leis on Memorial Day.

But in truth, Punchbowl's crosses were the exception in the national cemetery system and were never to be more than temporary markers until flat stones could be prepared and placed on the graves.

The Army had taken pains to explain this policy to the Honolulu media throughout the planning process. It sought to support the policy with a hurried survey among ten prominent community leaders on their preference for upright or flat markers. Only one of the ten said he preferred the crosses, but that one person—the editor of the largest daily newspaper in the state—became the vocal leader in the fight to save the crosses after the Army did what to many was the unthinkable:

It tore the crosses down.

Not unexpectedly, that action created a furor.

The Army had begun in the summer of 1951 to publicize its original intention to remove the crosses once all the graves had received their flat markers. In addition, a survey on the condition of the crosses showed that more than half the 13,000 in the cemetery needed to be replaced, at a cost of more than $3.50 each.

Hawaii's veterans organizations immediately took aim at the Army's so-called "economy move." One opponent said the removal of the crosses would make Punchbowl "look like a vacant lot." Veterans clubs passed resolutions and sent them to the Territory's delegate in Washington, urging Congressional action to save the crosses.

By now the Army was anxious to implement its original policy and when all the newly arrived flat headstones were in place the local commander ordered the crosses removed. The action occurred in a single morning, September 24, 1951.

Reaction was swift in coming, as local veterans organizations decried the removal. The news media picked up the story and reaction poured in from the Mainland. Francis Cardinal Spellman of New York called the Army's economic justification for the cross removal "deplorable." *The Houston Chronicle* editorialized that the action was "...one of the most disgraceful incidents of an era in which government has lost all perspective as to costs and values." The paper implied that "Communist-minded advisers" were behind a plot "to erase the names of the fallen and the record of their heroic deaths from their resting place..."

In the early months of the controversy Congressional resolutions were introduced and hearings were held in Washington in an effort supported by a relatively few members of Congress to replace the crosses. But as months and then years passed even that support dwindled. The controversy continued to receive newspaper editorial space in Honolulu, but the movement never gathered

enough momentum to challenge the Army's often-stated national cemetery grave marker policy. President Truman's public endorsement of the Army's actions at Punchbowl did much to diffuse the issue and ensure that the crosses would not again be raised at Puowaina.

Four years after the crosses were removed, Hawaii's delegate to Congress at the time, Mrs. Joseph R. Farrington, reflected on the grave marker issue:

"The idea of a national cemetery in Punchbowl was conceived on my lanai (patio) at Pacific Heights. My husband (who was then Hawaii's delegate to Congress), Robert O. Thompson, landscape architect, and I first thought up the idea looking down into Punchbowl...

"...we were the ones who agreed at that time that the flat markers would be most appropriate, not knowing at all that that was the policy of the Department of the Army for our national cemeteries. We were just modern-minded people, and I had just completed the design with Mr. Thompson for a flat marker for our family plot following the death of Joe's father, the late Governor Farrington.

"The real mistake was made when the temporary white crosses were erected in Punchbowl before the arrival of the flat markers. The impact on this scene is so impressive to the people of Hawaii that it has become very much of an issue...."

Few today, however, would question the

On May 15, 1958, four of Punchbowl's Korea "unknowns" were presented as candidates for interment in the Tomb of the Unknown Soldier at Arlington National Cemetery in Washington, D.C. Army Master Sgt. Ned Lyle, a decorated Korea veteran, was given the honor of making the selection.

removal of the upright markers. The emotional preference felt by many for the crosses is long gone among Hawaii's veterans and the survivors of those who lie here. The sense of religion represented by the upright crosses and Stars of David is found today on each headstone of the known burials in the form of an engraved cross, star or Buddhist wheel.

The controversy was lost, of course, on the men the grave markers—flat or upright— were meant to honor. More than 13,000 casualties of World War II were interred within a year's time at Punchbowl; 2,055 of them were "Unknowns"—men who could not be identified but whose bodies had been recovered for burial.

It was not long before other battles were sending home the bodies of young men to Punchbowl. Officially known as a "conflict" and not a war, Korea was just as deadly to

The text on the crate reads:

UNKNOWN X-2160 SB
KOKURA, AGRS, AFFE
FOR NAT'L MEMORIAL CEMETERY
OF THE PACIFIC
HONOLULU, HAWAII

18

35

HA-42-K

Above: An unknown soldier from
Korea is guided to his final rest.
Above right: One of America's first
casualties in the War of the Pacific.

those swept away by it, and a total of 1,242 killed in the Korean Conflict eventually were buried at Punchbowl.

Included among this number are 866 Unknowns. Punchbowl is the final resting place for all of the Korea Unknowns, nearly all of whom were buried between February and May of 1956. Two years later, on May 15, 1958, a selection was made by a decorated veteran of the Korean Conflict from among four of the Unknowns to determine which would be honored as the Unknown Soldier of the Korean Conflict at Arlington National Cemetery.

The Unknowns from World War II had been buried among their identified brothers in arms, but nearly all of the Korea Unknowns lie together as a bloc in Section U of the cemetery. The only times the distinction becomes obvious are on those special days of remembrance when families and friends decorate Punchbowl's graves with flower leis and bouquets. Not all graves are decorated on these days, but the absence of flowers on the graves of the Korea Unknowns in Section U is especially noticeable. Perhaps to compensate for the sense of loneliness one feels for the

Unknowns, floral offerings by clubs and organizations made to the National Memorial Cemetery of the Pacific are accepted on behalf of the Unknowns of all wars who are buried there.

From the beginning, plans for a national cemetery in Punchbowl contained a memorial to those who died in the Pacific Theater of World War II. With America's involvement in the Korean Conflict the scope of the project was broadened, and ground was broken on Memorial Day 1958 for the structure that today dominates the western end of the crater.

Unlike the Unknowns, who at least lie in graves known to their countrymen, tens of thousands of American fighting men from World War II and Korea died and never came home. They were missing in action or lost or buried at sea. For them, there would never be a grave for loved ones to decorate, for small children to visit with respect. Only this memorial would record the names of 18,093 Americans missing in the Central, Northern, Western and Southern Pacific regions of World War II. (Another 36,279 of the missing from the Southwestern Pacific would be

memorialized at the Manila American Military Cemetery in the Philippines.) All of Korea's 8,163 missing would be listed at Punchbowl.

The project, which originally was to be completed in five years, eventually would stretch out to eight. Even as the delays forced one dedication postponement after another, the memorial itself was becoming outdated. The United States had again become embroiled in another bloody Asian conflict, and again young Americans were dying. More graves would be filled at Punchbowl and new marble tablets would list the names of the missing in Vietnam.

---

*The rifles fired a final salute and "Taps" echoed across the crater of Punchbowl. The American flag was folded and handed to the next of kin. The mourners dispersed and silence settled once again on the calm morning.*

*It was a scene familiar to Punchbowl but there were differences. The dead were not casualties of a war being fought by a unified and united America. They had died in the jungles and highlands of an embattled country in Indochina, and many Americans were saying they should not have been there at all.*

*But they were there, as many as half a million of them at one time, and their battles suddenly dominated the world news and were brought by television into American living rooms. For the first time Americans who stayed home could witness the heroism, the tragedies and the waste of warfare. Unfamiliar names became commonplace—Saigon, Da Nang, Kontum, Quang Tri, Rung Sat, Binh Hoa. And the name of the nation itself, Vietnam, would be seared into the American consciousness.*

*The men who died there and are buried in Punchbowl came home to grieving families; they had fallen in combat and would be accorded all honors due men who had responded to their nation's call to arms. The rightness or wrongness of the Vietnam war was no longer their concern. That was now and forever left to their survivors.*

*A total of 213 Americans killed in action in Vietnam are buried in Punchbowl. Recognized as missing in action are another 2,489.*

*Today, among their comrades, they lie beyond any judgment on earth, having given no less of themselves than any soldier of any previous war America has fought. And the same sun that falls softly on other, older markers touches theirs, and the same wind out of the northeast passes over them all in an eternal benediction.*

---

Punchbowl's first Vietnam casualty was buried in 1962, before work on the memorial

to the dead of World War II and Korea was even finished. The $3 million memorial project, begun in 1958, was virtually completed five years later, but repeated delays in Italy in the preparation of the battle maps for the memorial's galleries postponed the dedication until May 1, 1966.

The Dedicatory Stone at the base of the stairs is the focal point of numerous wreath-laying ceremonies each year. The inscription reads: "In These Gardens Are Recorded the Names of Americans Who Gave Their Lives in the Service of Their Country and Whose Earthly Resting Place is Known Only to God."

Eight Courts of the Missing originally were constructed beside the central stairway that leads to the Court of Honor with its chapel and map galleries. The Courts' 12-foot-high walls of Italian Trani marble contain the names of 18,093 missing from World War II. Another 8,163 are listed as the missing from the Korean Conflict. Two half-courts were dedicated in 1980 at the foot of the stairway to honor 2,489 missing from Vietnam.

Below: Although all of the Korea missing are listed in the Courts, only about one-third of the missing from World War II's Pacific Theater are inscribed here. The rest are honored in the Philippines. Below right: The 30-foot high statue of Columbia gazes down upon the Court of Honor. Right: At the base of the statue is the message written by Abraham Lincoln to a mother whose five sons died in the Civil War.

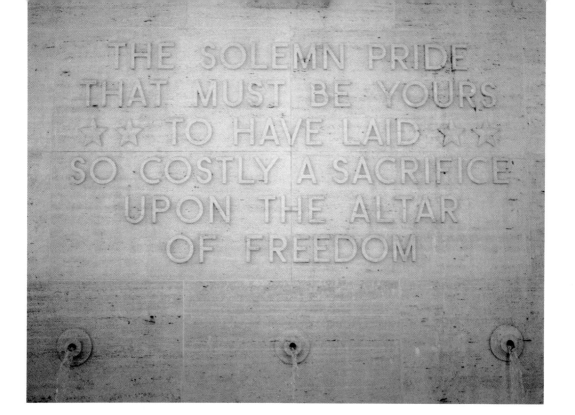

THE SOLEMN PRIDE
THAT MUST BE YOURS
☆☆ TO HAVE LAID ☆☆
SO COSTLY A SACRIFICE
UPON THE ALTAR
OF FREEDOM

Above left: The frieze above the map galleries records the names of World War II campaigns in the Pacific. Above right: The maps trace the step-by-step progress of the Pacific war that ultimately led to the defeat of the Japanese Empire. Far right: The original maps for the galleries were made in Italy using an ancient technique, which was no match for Hawaii's heat and humidity.

The names are listed alphabetically by service on the tablets. They represent every state of the Union and the District of Columbia, Puerto Rico, Guam, Samoa, the Philippines, the Panama Canal Zone, Mexico and Canada. (Page 64 contains a diagram showing the location of the memorial and its Courts of the Missing.)

Medal of Honor winners are designated in the courts by a gold star and gold lettering of the name. The tablets do not record the names of those interred in the cemetery. Information on grave locations can be obtained from the Administration Building at the cemetery's entrance.

The courts are shaded and surrounded by exotic tropical foliage, including a frangipani tree in the center of each. On the stairway side of the courts are white flowering monkeypod trees with allamanda shrubs. The outer sides of the courts contain a hedge of orange jessamine, as well as rainbow shower and Chinese banyan trees. Beds of cup-of-gold and star jasmine decorate the top of the slope.

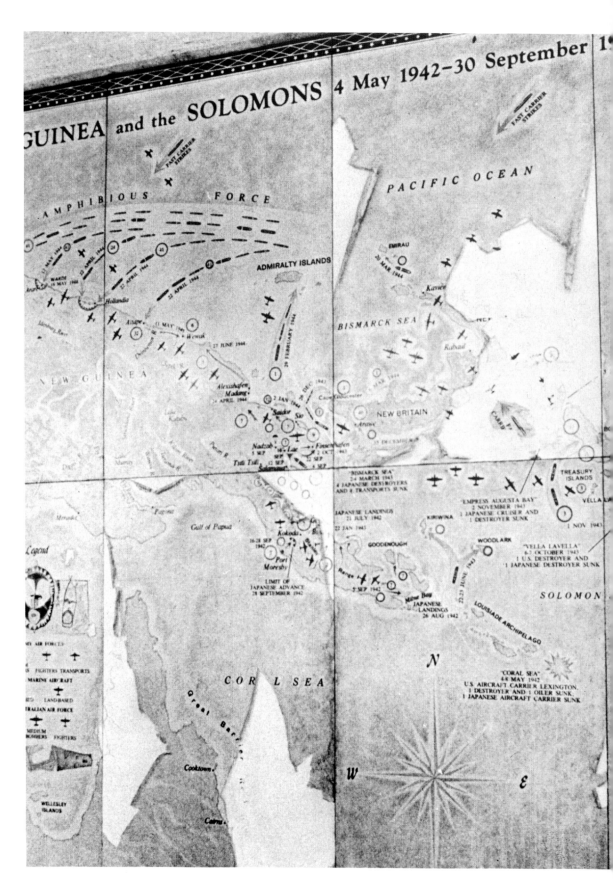

PACIFIC OCEAN

AMPHIBIOUS FORCE

FAST CARRIER STRIKES

ADMIRALTY ISLANDS

EMIRAU
20 MAR 1944

Kavien

BISMARCK SEA

Rabaul

NEW GUINEA

Alexishafen,
Madang
24 APRIL 1944

Cape Gloucester

Saidor
2 JAN 1944

Sio

NEW BRITAIN

Nadzab
5 SEP
Tsili Tsili
Lae
Finschhafen
2 OCT 1943
Salamaua 12 SEP

"BISMARCK SEA"
24 MARCH 1943
4 JAPANESE DESTROYERS
AND 8 TRANSPORTS SUNK

TREASURY
ISLANDS

VELLA LA

"EMPRESS AUGUSTA BAY"
2 NOVEMBER 1943
1 JAPANESE CRUISER AND
1 DESTROYER SUNK

KIRIWINA

1 NOV 1943

JAPANESE LANDINGS
21 JULY 1942
22 JAN 1943

Menari

GOODENOUGH

WOODLARK

"VELLA LAVELLA"
6-7 OCTOBER 1943
1 U.S. DESTROYER AND
1 JAPANESE DESTROYER SUNK

Gulf of Papua

Kokoda
16-28 SEP
1942
Buna

Port
Moresby

LIMIT OF
JAPANESE ADVANCE
28 SEPTEMBER 1942

Rango
5 SEP 1942

Milne Bay
JAPANESE
LANDINGS
26 AUG 1942

LOUISIADE ARCHIPELAGO

SOLOMON

Legend

CORAL SEA

Great Barrier

Cooktown

"CORAL SEA"
4-8 MAY 1942
U.S. AIRCRAFT CARRIER LEXINGTON,
1 DESTROYER AND 1 OILER SUNK,
1 JAPANESE AIRCRAFT CARRIER SUNK

N

W

E

WELLESLEY
ISLANDS

Cairns

**4** ON 24 JULY, AFTER A LENGTHY PREPARATORY BOMBARDMENT BY U.S. SHIPS, AIRCRAFT AND ARTILLERY FIRING FROM SAIPAN, THE 4TH MARINE DIVISION FOLLOWED BY THE 2D MARINE DIVISION LANDED ON NORTHERN TINIAN. AFTER NINE DAYS OF SEVERE FIGHTING, WITH CONTINUOUS SUPPORT BY SEVENTH AIR FORCE AND CARRIER AIRCRAFT AND BY NAVAL GUNFIRE, THE MARINES SECURED THE ISLAND.

FRONT LINES
U.S. ASSAULT FORCES
AIRCRAFT CARRIERS
LANDING SHIPS AND CRAFT
TRANSPORT AND CARGO SHIPS
FIRE SUPPORT SHIPS

U.S. ARMY AIR FORCES

HEAVY BOMBERS    MEDIUM BOMBERS    FIGHTERS

U.S. NAVY & MARINE AIRCRAFT

CARRIER-BASED    LAND-BASED

JAPANESE COUNTERATTACKS
AIRFIELDS

*Legend*

The Italian maps were replaced with new murals of concrete and colorful crushed glass.

The Court of Honor is dominated by the 30-foot statue of Columbia, signifying the United States of America, carrying a laurel branch and standing on the symbolized prow of an aircraft carrier. Beneath her are the words of sympathy written by President Abraham Lincoln to the mother of five sons killed during the Civil War: "The Solemn Pride That Must Be Yours to Have Laid So Costly A Sacrifice Upon the Altar of Freedom."

The sculpture and the eagles above the doorways to the map galleries were designed by Bruce Moore of Washington, D.C., and were carved by Filippo Cacchetti of Trivoli and Ugo Quaglieri of Rome, Italy. On the frieze of the galleries are some of the memorable places where Americans fought and died with honor in the Pacific and Asia: PEARL HARBOR * CORAL SEA * MID-WAY * ATTU * SOLOMONS * GILBERTS * MARSHALLS * MARIANAS * LEYTE * IWO JIMA * OKINAWA * TOKYO * KOREA.

Inside the galleries are the ten maps that detail the progress of the war against the Japanese Empire and two maps of the major battle actions in the Korean Conflict. The maps displayed here today are not those originally prepared in Italy for the memorial. The first maps were created by a process called scagliola, a technique dating back to Biblical times. A paste consisting of marble dust and a special cement was applied to Carrara marble. Pigments were added as well as a sealing glaze, and the entire surface was polished to a mirror finish.

The Italian artisans in Florence who created the maps said the scagliola paintings would "last forever and a day." But Hawaii's humidity, heat and sea air were too much for the delicate creation, and within three years large segments of the maps had peeled from the marble. The American Battle Monuments Commission, which supervised the construction and still administers the memorial, ordered the complete replacement of the Italian maps, and new murals of concrete and crushed colored glass were installed. The murals have stood well the test of Hawaii's

elements and their brightly colored glass of contrasting shades are considered an improvement over the soft pastels of the original maps.

The 32-seat chapel behind the central tower of the memorial provides a cool refuge from the glare of Hawaii's tropical sun. The colored glass "cabochons" set into the doors, windows and altar rail of the chapel represent seven different symbols—Liberty, The Hero, The Hand of God, The Holy Dove, The Torch, The Lamb and The Shofar. Most of them are repeated several times in different colors. The Star of David, Buddhist Wheel and Christian Cross at the front of the chapel represent the religious preference of nearly all who are interred in Punchbowl. These symbols are engraved on the individual headstones throughout the cemetery.

The vestibule bears this dedicatory inscrip-

Left: The chapel, decorated here for Memorial Day, is a place for quiet reflection. Above: The Hero—one of seven colored glass symbols on the doors, windows and altar rail of the chapel.

IN PROUD REMEMBRANCE
OF THE ACHIEVEMENTS
OF HER SONS
AND IN HUMBLE TRIBUTE
TO THEIR SACRIFICES
THIS MEMORIAL
HAS BEEN ERECTED
BY
THE UNITED STATES OF AMERICA
1941-1945 ★ 1950-1953

Left: Grillwork in the chapel with its
glass "cabochons." Above:
Inscription in the chapel vestibule.

tion: "In Proud Remembrance of the Achievements of Her Sons and in Humble Tribute to
Their Sacrifices This Memorial Has Been
Erected by The United States of America
1941-1945 * 1950-1953." The American Battle
Monuments Commission had plans to in-
scribe the dates of the Vietnam Conflict as this
book was published.

The cemetery, War Memorial and overlook
of Honolulu at Punchbowl have combined to
make the crater Hawaii's most popular tourist
destination. In 1980 nearly 2.6 million people
visited Punchbowl, about 400,000 more than
the number of visits to the *U.S.S. Arizona*
Memorial at Pearl Harbor.

Each day, tour buses by the dozen drive
slowly through the cemetery gates and park at

Above: Hundreds of Scouts decorate Punchbowl's graves each Memorial Day. Above right: Hawaii's many ethnic groups have their own unique ways to honor their loved ones. Below right: Punchbowl's popular overlook attracts visitors from around the world.

the memorial, giving their passengers a few moments to inspect the Courts of the Missing, the battle maps and the memorial's chapel. Many walk the short distance to Ernie Pyle's grave. Other buses drive immediately to the overlook, passing tunnels in the crater's rim now used to store equipment. They are said to have been repositories during World War II for currency and other valuables.

From the overlook visitors have a sweeping and unbroken view of Honolulu and the southern portion of Oahu, from Diamond Head to Barbers Point and the Waianae

Mountains, out beyond Honolulu International Airport and Pearl Harbor.

A visit to Punchbowl can be a moving experience any time of the year, but there are a few days when the experience can be especially beautiful.

Punchbowl's annual Easter Sunrise Service, which has grown steadily in popularity since that first Sunday school class gathered there early this century, now attracts thousands of Hawaii residents and visitors. On Memorial Day each grave in the cemetery bears a small American flag and is decorated with flower leis strung by schoolchildren. More than 100 flags line the road leading to the memorial along the central mall. The flags once covered the caskets of those buried here and elsewhere and have been donated to the cemetery for this purpose. The "Avenue of Flags" also is displayed on Presidents Day, Independence Day, Veterans Day and Thanksgiving.

Thanksgiving. Beyond the beauty of Punchbowl, beyond the mandatory tourist stop at the overlook, beyond the curiosity—there is the thanksgiving.

In a real way, every day is Thanksgiving at

Punchbowl, as thankful prayers are offered by grateful Americans to those who fought and died for their country. And what veteran of World War II, Korea or Vietnam hasn't muttered a prayer of thanks that he, too, does not lie here at the Hill of Sacrifice?

The beauty and peace of Punchbowl live in the memory of visitors long after they return to their homes. But it would be sad if Punchbowl's greater significance were lost on those who come here from around the world.

The thousands of Americans who are buried or memorialized here represent only a fraction of the millions of people who have been consumed by the flames of war in this century—from the conflagrations of the World Wars to "police actions," "conflicts" and the assorted "brush fires" in most nations of the world.

Punchbowl—a Hill of Sacrifice in ancient and modern Hawaii—is a place to remember the innumerable individual sacrifices in all these wars and the collective loss we have suffered as an international brotherhood of man.

Perhaps in the remembering we will move closer to the end of war.

---

*Born in a paroxysm of explosions that changed the shape of the land, the tuff cone was unremarkable among its neighboring ranges until the coming of the first people. Human events and human values changed the cone forever, from a nameless landmark to Puowaina, the hill of the laying up of sacrifices; from Punchbowl and its guns to America's National Memorial Cemetery of the Pacific.*

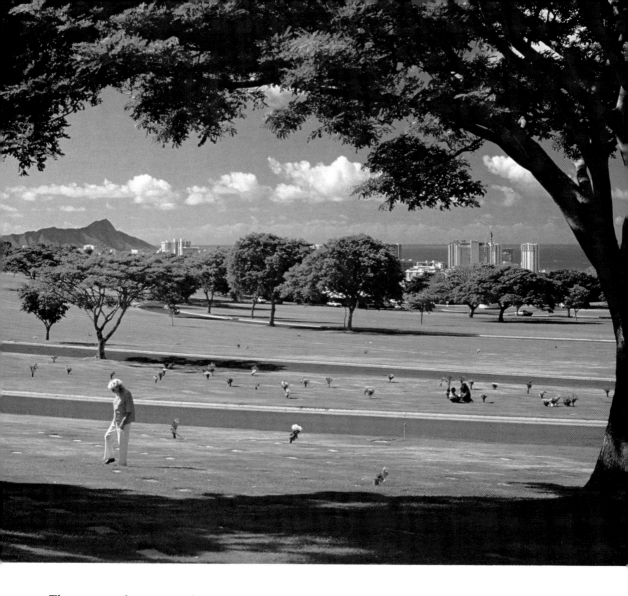

There are other national cemeteries but *Punchbowl is a special place, where legends and history freely mingle, and where the fitting symbolism has been a constant in a sea of variables. Punchbowl exists today not only as a resting place for those who died and are buried there, but as a reminder of their sacrifice.*

*It is a fitting place of rest. Now, as then, it remains above the noise and confusion of the life around it. The splendid silence is broken only by the wind that pushes easily across the expanse of crater or by the final rites for another whose remains will lie forever in the comradeship of others. There is a great calm beauty in the surrounding peaks and comfort in the gentle, flowering plants.*

*Through the centuries the Hill of Sacrifice has evolved, becoming finally a place of peace.*

Above left: A young man pauses on Memorial Day. Above: Puowaina—a place of peace.

# THE NATIONAL MEMORIAL CEMETERY OF THE PACIFIC
## 2177 Puowaina Drive, Honolulu, Hawaii 96813

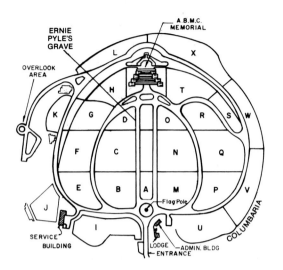

**Capsule Chronology:**

| | |
|---|---|
| **August 1948** | Construction begins |
| **January 4, 1949** | First interments |
| **July 19, 1949** | Gates open to public |
| **September 2, 1949** | Cemetery dedication (4th anniversary of VJ Day) |
| **May 1, 1966** | Memorial dedication |

**Statistics:**

| | |
|---|---|
| **Land area** | 114.54 acres |
| **Burial plots** | All of the approximately 30,000 plots were expected to be filled by late 1987. Columbaria to accommodate 4,800 cremated remains were added in 1982 to extend the cemetary's life 20 years. |

**Names inscribed in Courts of the Missing:**

| | |
|---|---|
| World War II | 18,093 |
| Korean Conflict | 8,163 |
| Vietnam Conflict | 2,489 |

**Eligibility for interment:** Any honorably discharged veteran or active member of the Armed Forces and his or her dependents.

**Hours of Operation
(seven days a week):**

**October 1 to February 28**
8:00 a.m. to 5:30 p.m.

**March 1 to September 30**
8:00 a.m. to 6:30 p.m.

**Longer hours in effect Easter and Memorial Day.**

---

## ACKNOWLEDGEMENTS

**Punchbowl** is dedicated to America's sons and daughters who are remembered at Puowaina.

Special appreciation to Tai-pan and Company for its invaluable contributions, and to Herman Wouk; Irwin Malzman; Buck Buchwach and the Hawaii Newspaper Agency; Honolulu Publishing Co., Ltd.; the Bernice P. Bishop Museum; the American Battle Monuments Commission; the United States Army; the United States Navy; the Veterans Administration and the staff of the National Memorial Cemetery of the Pacific.

## CREDITS

**Black and white photography:** Early photos on pages 15, 16, 17 and 18 from Bernice P. Bishop Museum. Pages 14, 22, 23, 39, 40, 41, 45 and 53 from Hawaii Newspaper Agency. Pages 26-27 and top of 37 courtesy of Department of the Navy, Public Affairs Office. Pages 30, 32, 33, 34, 35, 36, 37 (bottom), 42, 44 and 46 courtesy Department of the Army.

**Color photography:** Back cover from Loye Guthrie. Front cover and pages 11 (top), 24, 25, 28, 29, 31, 43, 47, 48, 50, 51 (top), 52, 54, 55, 56, 57, 58, 59, 60, 61 (top) and 62 from Brett Uprichard/Honolulu Publishing. Page 8 from Allan Seiden. Pages 1, 2, 3, 9, 10, 11 (bottom), 19, 20-21, 49, 50-51 (bottom), 61 (lower) and 63 from Werner Stoy/Camera Hawaii.
Pages 6 and 26-27 (bottom) courtesy of Worldwide Distributors.
Original art on pages 7, 12-13 and 17 by Franklin Luke.